RV LIVING IS A COOL SMART WAY TO LIVE, WORK & PLAY

BY PENNY SMART

ESCAPE THE RAT RACE TO JOIN THE LIFESTYLE

PENNY SMART

Editing: Joan and Bill Dalton

ISBN 9-781481-898102

First edition 2013

TABLE OF CONTENTS

PENNY SMART

Acknowledgements

Dedicated to my family - my husband Ed who is always there for me and my daughter Lonnie, who is one of the most loving and giving persons that I know.

Dedicated to my mentors - my father, my friends Sylvia & Joel, they are no longer physically here to share their stories & laughter and taught me to take chances in life, to follow my heart and I am forever grateful. Thank you to my cheering team, Agnes, Mary, Angela, Christina, Julie, Shelly, Sherry, Marilyn, Carol, Kerri, Lori, Carol, Sue, Debbie, Heather, Lisa, Don, Gail and God who has given me some wonderful gifts in life.

Special thanks to our fellow RVer friends Bill & Joan, George & Betty, Jeff &Rachel along with the many friends at Cyprus Woods who shared their fun experiences and insights on the RV lifestyle.

Support to my cause in life - 10% of all royalties will be donated to community mental health not for profit charities.

Penny Smart

Introduction

The cool lifestyle of an RVer has improved dramatically through the years. Now we can connect through the internet and use smartphone apps to do everyday tasks, such as working, banking, paying bills, shopping, communicating, schooling and more. Before now, it was impossible to do these things without a physical presence. This has led to the balanced lifestyle of today; comfortable travelling, living, working, and playing all while saving money.

The RVer's lifestyle is no longer just for those who have retired but for many who still continue to work or telecommute within this flexible environment. There are currently 1.3 million Americans that are full-time RVers and it continues to grow as more people see the cost benefits provided by opting out of mortgaged luxury for a simpler freedom lifestyle with a little or no debt.

A cool RVer's best companion is a smartphone (or tablet) that can assist with managing time and help save money in various ways because it works like a compact computer that you can carry in your back pocket or purse.

They are easy to use and, if your smart phone is Wi-Fi enabled, there are many cost saving features that can be utilized.

Using a mobile device can get overwhelming as there are thousands of applications to choose from and it can get noisy, but stay with me and master the basics first to gain extra time and then learn how to save money, so that we can invest in the things that we enjoy the most.

In this book, I will share the story of our transition to RV living and how we used internet technology to help us. There are many tips here that you can use from my years of being a internet geek who loves to have fun, RVing and helping others to make their lives simple.

Happy RVing!

PENNY SMART

"You are the Masterpiece of your own life & dreams"

OUR FIRST RV

"You've gotta dance like there's nobody watching,
Love like you'll never be hurt,
Sing like there's nobody listening,
And live like it's heaven on earth."
—William W. Purkey

We had operated a seasonal tourism business and enjoyed the RV life as part-time vacationers for 11 years before embarking on the lifestyle change of doing this full time.

What I mean as "full-time" is living in an RV all year round while still physically working in the summer season and then working remotely with our

---

business/marketing plan in the south during the winter season, which is our off season.

It all seems like history when in 2002, we used our savings to purchase our first RV, a 1988 used 28ft Georgie Boy.

It was a dream for us, a nicely furnished RV with a pullout couch, 2 TVs, a kitchen with dining area, washroom with shower and a small bedroom with queen-sized bed. The outside body showed weathered travel use, but it was a fixer upper so we got a good deal and Ed, my husband, is a good handy man.

When you walked in, it looked more like a furnished bus without seats and with custom windows but with a push of a button, the sides would expand and a comfortable living and dining area would suddenly appear that could accommodate four people.

Wow, Ed and I thought, how much more high tech could you get than that?

That was then and this is now. New technology advancements, such as Wi-Fi and the Internet, and smart phones, has resulted in a relaxed lifestyle that has revolutionized RVing.

RVing the Cool Lifestyle Way
Our First RV

The opportunities to travel, work and play with a RV are becoming common as more people than ever are discovering this wonderful way of living and travelling across the globe.

We had enjoyed our first older dream home on wheels for 2 years and then began upgrading every few years, gradually moving up to our latest RV, a 36ft Holiday Rambler Motor Coach.

It was a novel adventure, being able to escape almost instantly with this place we called "our condo on wheels" parked in our driveway.

With the luxuries of a real home on wheels we found it a really exciting way to travel that certainly exceeded our expectations, a thought echoed by many who have embraced this lifestyle.

With our vehicle in action, we started going away on weekends for camping trips and taking short holiday trips to Florida.

Our first crossover through the USA border with such a large vehicle was very intimidating at first but it became easier each time and we noted that as long as you had your passport, destination address along with your directions and any other required documentation there is no problem. We have found it is best to travel at night when there are no line ups at the border.

If you start travelling across the border often, you may want to consider getting a Canadian Nexus Pass[i] or American Nexus Pass[ii] for a fee which prequalifies you as low risk, making it quicker to go across the border.

To our surprise, we did have a minor incident once, where the subs and the beef in our fridge were confiscated by a border officer as there was a cross border beef ban.

After that, we now travel with an empty fridge and I would recommend that you do the same when crossing the border. You also learn to travel lightly stocked in order to save on fuel costs.

Once we arrived at our various resort destinations after staying overnight in rest stops, we discovered modern conveniences and that I could take my work anywhere as many of the resorts had Wi-Fi access. Even when we went camping at some national parks, we were pleasantly surprised to learn that they had electrical outlets at some sites and I could work for a few hours by tapping into the office remotely with

RVing the Cool Lifestyle Way

Our First RV

GoToMyPC[iii] in the morning and then relax in beautiful surroundings in the afternoon. I laugh as I remember the one time we had a pizza delivered to our campfire in the middle of nowhere.

With Wi-Fi access, I could phone, fax and have Web-Conferences[iv] through my computer and no one would know if I was in Canada or not.

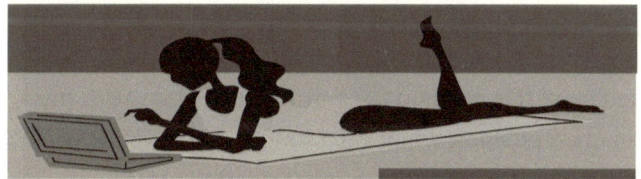

I found that many of these internet business services are free for an initial trial period and then the cost is very affordable to maintain afterwards.

There were many times international and business calls were made early in the morning in order to keep my afternoons free. Of course, I could not miss taking important calls, so to maintain balance, I would call forward my phone in the afternoon to E-voice [v] a voice

---

answering service, which would translate all calls to text and email them to me with a special tone.

I would then schedule mini blocks of time to reply to the business emails.

In keeping the RV organized and not wanting it to look like an office, I travelled light with my office being only my laptop, smartphone, scanner and headset. I used Myfax[vi] to receive and send faxes through my computer and my headset for phone calls on Skpye[vii]. Everything fitted neatly into my briefcase, which I put away once I finished.

I had used this method for a number of years with my executive position while vacationing in the RV. Now as a full-timer, I feel that I am on a vacation after I complete my work day and love this lifestyle which is far from our reality of eleven years ago.

Before we had educated ourselves on RVs, we used to wonder how one can afford to buy and live in a gas guzzling RV home that could cost more than $100,000.00 as we had seen at the RV shows.

We had thought that the people who owned RVs must have been wealthy with good disposable income to afford this type of lifestyle.

RVing the Cool Lifestyle Way
Our First RV

We discovered that this was a myth. We found that there is an RV for every type of budget and living economics that are no different than purchasing a starter home in your neighbourhood of choice, only with an RV you can move away in an hour if you don't like your neighbours. As a full-timer it is normally less expensive to live in an RV than in regular housing.

The majority of RV purchasers usually start off with small steps either renting one or purchasing a used one to see if this is to their liking. Some find that it is not really for them while others enjoy the sense of freedom and work towards purchasing one.

You can start with a fixer up like we did and, if you are looking for a bargain, you can usually get good prices at public auctions, distress classifieds or car dealers that have taken a trade in for a car and have had an RV sitting in their lot for a while. There is always a deal available, if you have cash on hand and are willing to wait for the right opportunity.

My word of advice is to research any perspective RVs if you are going to use this route. Get the RV inspected thoroughly by a mechanic who knows about RVs

---

before making that big decision, ensure that it has no liens or accident history and try to get the service maintenance records, as they normally don't come with any warranties unless you are buying from a dealer. And if the deal is too good to be true, it probably is, so be wary and careful.

It took us a year before we made a decision to buy our first used one. The best route is to purchase one from a reputable dealer as there are warranties and other extras that are usually thrown in. Dealers will also offer some good financing options similar to buying a house with some loan terms as long as 20 years.

Economically when you weigh out the cost, it can work out to being no different than paying for an annual vacation or purchasing a cottage, it all depends on how much you spend on vacations.

For us, it was very comforting to be travelling on the road in a home-like setting rather than flying cramped up to reach a destination. With an RV, you are home no matter where you go, and there are thousands of places still to explore in North America with plenty of places where you can stay.

For us, travelling with our pets was the biggest benefit and we found the freedom to do so is worth its weight in gold.

Figure 1 -Our travelling Chihuahuas

Penny Smart

SECOND THOUGHTS

"You only live once, but if you do it right, once is enough."
— Mae West

With our first RV purchase, we initially thought it was an expensive cost for just a few weekends to escape and a couple weeks of holidays a year with having such a large vehicle parked in our driveway and to pay for insurance when not used.

After long and heated discussions, we decided to justify our negative thoughts with a "why should we list".

PROS OF WHY WE SHOULD KEEP RV LIST:

_____

RVing the Cool Lifestyle Way
Tips for Financing

- ➢ Emergency home for power outages, disasters & survival with generator

- ➢ Quick self –contained escape on wheels

- ➢ Can take our pets with us

- ➢ No packing and unpacking on vacations

- ➢ Washroom access where ever we are travelling

- ➢ Almost same cost of an annual vacation

- ➢ Exploring North America

We certainly got hooked in this life after a few years as we discovered a fascinating world with RV living in resorts and campgrounds, a world with a beautiful sense of community and friendliness at every place that we ventured too. There were no second thoughts after we compiled our list.

TIPS FOR FINANCING

"Wall Street is the only place that people drive to in a Rolls Royce to take advice from people who ride the subway."
— Warren Buffet

We discovered that the best time to buy an RV is during off-season when business is slow for the dealers or at a RV show.

Do a Google[1] search to find where local RV shows are being hosted and start by attending some as you will get insider information and tips on the industry. We found the competition is fierce during these shows and it works to your advantage in negotiating as

[1] www.google.com is an internet search tool to assist you in finding or locating items by typing in a word or phrase.

dealers would rather sell than transport the inventory back to stock.

Before purchasing an RV, there are some simple tips to keep in mind. Namely, you need to make sure that when you apply for financing that you can service the debt and have at least 10 to 20% down.

We had used our RV as a trade in and moved up each time.

Be prepared as financiers will look at key indicators to evaluate risk before lending you funds to purchase your RV, they will look at your credit score and net-worth which consists of the assets you own less any liabilities money that you owe to ensure that you are not over extended. They will assess your ability to pay back the debt as you will need to show stability such as permanent address and steady income.

Some dealers can work with you and may have more favourable options than going directly to a financial institution that is more restrictive.

Penny Smart

If you are planning to convert to a full-time RV lifestyle get everything in order first, even if it takes you a year or two.

You can run a free credit score on yourself through Equifax[viii] to see your credit position and get it corrected if there are inaccuracies.

It will be difficult to finance anything if you are transient and living mobile with little or no income or a dedicated residential address.

However, there are always places that will offer financing with higher than normal interest rates for those who qualify.

One reason to become a full-timer RVer is try to save money and reduce debt, so it may be best to rent for a while before digging yourself in a deep hole.

Many of the full-time RVers that we have come across had sold their home and used a good portion of that money to make a down payment so that they would have very little debt. The full-timer RV lifestyle is about being debt-free and having a sense of freedom.

Other alternatives would be using a home equity line of credit if you own a home and still want to keep both.

Tips for financing an RV:

➢ Have at least 10-20% down

➢ Get financing in place while you a have home and a steady income in place

➢ Pull up your credit history through Equifax

➢ Have a good debt to income ratio – use Google to assist in finding a calculator

➢ Good credit scores can negotiate better interest rates

➢ Determine the payments that you can afford and what you need monthly

➢ Amortization periods can be longer – find out from dealer the best terms.

PENNY SMART

> ➤ Go to your normal banking institution to see if they can give you a better interest rate.

Figure 2 - RVing in high end resorts

RV LIFESTYLE

The secret of happiness is freedom, the secret of freedom is courage."
— Carrie Jones

Whenever you venture to a RV resort, you can feel the innocence of childhood emotions that are re-captured by adults who enjoy having fun. You hear laughter and happiness. Every resort is unique with its own events and activities.

Some resorts are gated and are owned by the residents. You may see an active community with people riding their bikes, walking, playing tennis or shuffle boards, doing team activities and living everyday as it comes—there is a strong sense of safety and enjoyment in these communities.

Once you start RVing, it's like you belong to a special club and when you are in travel mode you give the fraternal wave or nod while passing each other on the highway.

You would think that RV life is one of the best kept secrets for a lifestyle change for full-time living, but it's not. RVing has been around since 1914[ix] .

When I started researching and looking up everything about RVing I came across a classic movie from 1954, which I would recommend that you see online or purchase called the Long, Long Trailer with Lucille Ball and Desi Arnez, it is humorous version of RVing and mobile living in the 50's. Every time I see it, I laugh hard as much really hasn't changed except for technology and upgrades, which makes RVing today a simpler and cooler lifestyle.

According to the University of Michigan's 2011 RV study, it's a trend that's growing, with large numbers of people looking to untether themselves from their homes and seek new adventures. And it's a lifestyle that's not just for retirees. The typical RV owner is 48 years old, with the largest gains in ownership in the 35 to 54 age bracket.[2]

Another demographic shift in RVing is more business people adapting to a telecommuting lifestyle just like we have done. This change is made possible by the accessibility of the internet combined with smartphones. If you do a quick search on YouTube for RVing, you will also see a younger generation such as students and young adults sharing tips and experiences on this type of lifestyle called cheap living they call it greening or living off the grid.

There are other full time RVers, who choose not to live permanently in any location and travel from place to place by dry camping and parking for days or weeks for free, then moving on to the next place once their welcome is overextended. An RV is equipped to be self-sufficient with their own generator and water system and some will have solar panels installed to save even more on costs to live as frugal as possible.

1. White Paper from President Richard Coon, Recreation Vehicle Industry, October 2011.

To stay connected they use their WiFi enabled Smartphone or tablet or may purchase a portable MIFI device to connect to the internet that creates a private hot spot that will travel with them anywhere.

 You will see these type of RVers in big box store parking lots, casinos, industrial areas, on residential streets, churches, public parks or anywhere where parking is allowed overnight, similar to a Transport truck staying overnight in an area.

Another way of RV living is boondocking, think of how the cowboys used to live way back when with their travels and camping experiences. Boondocking means RV camping in rural and remote country side areas without any hook ups to live self- sufficiently or off the grid in natural settings such as in national forests, state parks, in the desert or in vacant military bases and areas away from other campers and sites.

Some people enjoy this type of lifestyle to be in natural surroundings and be away from civilization as much as possible. While some cannot afford to live this lifestyle without earning an income, they can access a site called Workamper [3] as some of the

---

[3] http://www.workamper.com/

RVing the Cool Lifestyle Way

Disappearing in 90 days

National Parks will offer free living in exchange for working with a combination of wages. RV living is all about how you want to create your own lifestyle by design.

As an RVer you start to learn a lot about the industry and lingo as there are three different types of RVs [x] to choose from that can be matched to various budgets and lifestyle.

1. Motorhomes which are drivable living quarters

2. Towables which need to be towed by a vehicle

3. Truck Campers which sit on top of a truck

Within these categories, they are separated into various classifications and types, which you can do a Google search to find out more information on the dozens of variations.

My quick definition is a condo on wheels and boutique camping in beautiful surroundings.

PENNY SMART

It was a joy for us to be able to take our two pet Chihuahuas with us on our travels at all times. As empty nesters, they became the little ones in our lives and give us joy daily.

We have had the pleasure of vacationing across Canada with our RV as well as travelling to southern Florida for the past 11 years. If you have not been to Florida or any travel destination before, do a Google search with your destination as the keyword "tourism", for example "Florida tourism"[4] and it will bring you to all the tourism related items for that destination. These sites are usually government run and have good coupon offers to encourage tourism in their state or province.

During our initial years we enjoyed various resort campgrounds and travelling around until we decided that if we were to do this full-time, we needed two destinations that we could call our home base with being one in Canada and the other one in Florida, keeping in mind that we could not stay outside Ontario for more than 180 days annually due to residency and income tax laws.

---

[4] http://www.visitflorida.com/

RVing the Cool Lifestyle Way

Disappearing in 90 days

By staying in a destination, such as an RV resort, for a period of time it helped us to feel settled as there is a period of adjustment once you convert to full-time. It does take a while to get used to living in smaller quarters and to feel like part of the resort community. Having previously lived in a small condo, I found that it is comparable feeling as you learn to use the available facilities that are spread outside rather than inside your unit.

There are permanent RVers that stay parked in the community long term and don't leave as well as those that are transient.

In renting a RV lot, you can get a better deal by staying more than a month as it takes time to do hook ups, set up satellite and internet services, and mail forwarding, so it is more cost effective to stay longer in one place and negotiate for a longer term. Many full-timers will eventually purchase a lot when they find a location that they want to settle into.

If you do enjoy the adventure lifestyle and boutique camping at various destinations without having a home base, you can expect to pay anywhere from

---

Penny Smart

$30.00 to $55.00 night, which is average pricing or you can stay in temporary places such as Wal-Mart parking lots, rest stops and truck stops that have no charge and no hook ups while travelling. Belonging to RV memberships clubs, which start at $40.00, can also get you discounted rates and free stays.

Before setting out on your travels you may want to do some homework and research on the internet first and then follow-up by phoning your destination to reserve a place.

Although we find smartphones are good for information, there are areas where you may travel to that may have a small blackout area where there is no cellular access, so be prepared and have information that is printed or saved on your tablet.

We have found that being a member of CAA RV Plus[xi] (Canadian Automobile Association, the Canadian equivalent of Triple AAA,[xii] American Automobile Association) has been invaluable to us, especially when our RV has broke down over the years and needed towing or gas.

The membership has paid for itself many times over and has many benefits and cost savings. I consider it an investment rather than a membership. The

---

association also has a service called Trip Tik, where they will map out the route to your destination and send you maps that show all the rest stops along the way. If you have a particular type of RV, there are also manufacturers memberships that you can join that offer valuable tips and forums to assist owners if there are any problems. You are never alone when you own a RV as other RVers like to help one another.

I would also recommend the Good Sam Club[xiii] for a US membership, as they have campground ratings and discounts for Camping World[5] which is one of my favorite places for getting everything you need for your RV, plus RV forums and useful information for RVers –you get more than your money's worth for the membership cost.

The other resources that are available for a small fee will provide a physical directory and can also advise you of campgrounds, resorts and location ratings from other RVers such as Woodall's Campground Guide[xiv], and Passport America.[xv]   However, we have been to

[5] http://www.campingworld.com/

some campgrounds that were rated high and we were disappointed when we arrived as the reviews were quite out of date. I would recommend that you try to read current reviews on the internet through a Google search first. Current reviews of campgrounds are also starting to appear in Trip Advisor[6], which has ratings and travel reviews where you can search and rate any travel, restaurant and hotel experience.

All these memberships are also available to download at the App store and can be searched for by name as I explain in the smartphones chapter.

Travel Plazas are good places for RVers as stops and are located just off the highways. They are normally open 24 hours and they have clean facilities for staying overnight, showering, eating, gas, coffee and retail shops that are geared for the travellers. They had originally catered to truckers but with the growth of RVers, they have grown to accommodate both types of travellers.

When we occasionally break down, we can go to a Truck Stop Plaza that has Truck mechanic stations nearby for minor repairs. We have had good

---

[6] http://www.tripadvisor.com/

---

experiences and dealt with pretty honest mechanics that have saved us money.

Advance planning works best because with such a large vehicle you don't want to find out after arriving that they don't have any space or cannot accommodate you as maneuvering around can sometimes be difficult and planning your route beforehand is the best course of action.

If your route is long, you may consider stops where temporary overnight staying is allowed for free, such as rest stops that are located on the highway and also Wal-Mart parking lots, which you can research on the internet beforehand.

The Allstays app has helped us identify which Wal-Marts allow for overnight stays, because in some towns it may be against local by-laws.

Our preferred method of travel is a RV Resort as a final destination, where you have all the amenities available for a comfortable home lifestyle as a full-time RVer.

PENNY SMART

I like to refer to staying at an RV resort as "Boutique Living" because some of the resorts that we have stayed at have been like living in a hotel with Olympic size pools, Jacuzzis, exercise rooms, laundry facilities, licensed bars with entertainment, security, with active daily programs.

While we are not experts with this new lifestyle, having only been to around two dozen RV Resorts, we have learned a lot and found that each one is different.

Some of these resorts will have an ownership run similar to condominiums with a board of directors that have voting rights, a property manager on site, and rules and regulations that are posted on line.

A good resort will have an activity director with monthly posted activities and weekly breakfast meetings welcoming new people. If you have been on cruise excursions with activities, it would be a scaled down versions of their programs.

Each resort is different with their offerings and programs. Before staying at one you can also view comments and reviews from past guests by doing a Google search or requesting a copy of their activity calendar. Some of the resorts will charge just as much as a hotel stay as it is all based on the amenities and management or owner of the lot.

Remember that choosing these resorts is no different than selecting the best neighbourhood or hotel that you may want to stay in. You can select budget living and camping with no frills to upscale living with all amenities and manicured lots that have perfectly lined palm trees and landscaping that intermingles RV lots with full-time mobile home residents.

With most of these resorts, you can usually purchase or lease a lot for your RV and pay annual maintenance fees or have a small mortgage on the lot.

Some also have various rental packages that you can obtain from the property management corporations that are acting on behalf of the owners or from the owners directly.

In Florida, it is interesting to note that some resorts may be age restricted, such as 55 plus communities or only cater to retirees and still not have internet access.

PENNY SMART

With the trend of the full-time RV living growing in younger generations, there will be more resorts developed in the future to accommodate this need and demand.

Most of these resorts are pet friendly and some of the higher-end resorts do have restrictions on the year and type of RV that will be allowed on the premises, in order to keep with the resort standards and look.

With budget type resorts, they may be intermingled with tent campground facilities and may not have a community centre with other amenities and may be run by a corporation rather than individual ownership. In the higher-end ownership resorts which are gated and secure, it is not usual to see an RV in the price range of a million dollars or more, with a Porsche, BMV or another expensive vehicle parked beside it.

Most have lot sizes that are just enough to hold your RV and some space for lounging and eating, however, some lots may be more spacious than others as you are living in very close quarters to your neighbour.

It is always best to do research first before staying at a resort to ensure that it fits with your lifestyle and can accommodate your needs.

RVing the Cool Lifestyle Way

Disappearing in 90 days

With full-time RVing, it is certainly a lifestyle adjustment and you quickly learn that you can save a lot of money by not paying for a huge mortgage, utilities, and other home expenses.

You can stretch your financial resources more with careful budgeting and learn from other RVers who have mastered good budgeting and financial management over the years.

The lifestyle cost is really up to you with how you budget and your comfort level needed to feel safe and secure.

When we came back from our last vacation of three months in 2012, we parked the RV in our driveway and when we opened the door of our home, we were welcomed by the smell of a musty unlived in and empty house.

As empty nesters, we no longer felt that our home of 25 years was a cozy place anymore. It was a waste of our money to pay for a mortgage, security and maintenance help while we were away.

Our daughter was grown up and my father was no longer living with us. It just didn't make sense financially. That was when we had an "AHA" moment where we decided to take the leap to become full-timers.

Disappearing in 90 Days

"To be free, to be happy and fruitful, can only be attained through sacrifice of many common and but overestimated things"
–Robert Henry

Once we made the decision that we were going to change our lifestyle, the next step was how to do it.

Do we sell our house or rent it out?

We made the decision to rent out our home as it would be used as our retirement pool and could still appreciate with the housing market being soft. The onus would be finding a good tenant.

To our advantage, there were some local RV resorts in the neighbourhood that we could live at while we rented our house and worked at our seasonal summer business that requires us to be stationary for about 7 months.

During the other 5 months, we could work virtually and manage our operations anywhere with internet access. No sweat we thought and then we looked around.

With a 2,000 square foot 3 bedroom house that was filled with décor, furnishings, games, clothes, artwork, antiques and walk-in closets with over 30 years of accumulated time together, with my daughter's, father's, niece's belongings that had all previously lived with us, I would say that we were borderline hoarders with overstocked clutter.

The irony is that after they all left, when we should have downsized, we just bought more stuff to fill the emptiness not thinking that we would ever leave.

PENNY SMART

What would we do with it all?

We needed to purge to get rid of 2,000 square feet of stuff to fit into our new living space of 340 square feet that was sitting in our driveway.

That meant a living adjustment of down to 17% or 1660 less square feet.

This would be challenging as our seasonal business would be in full operation by June, which gave us less than 90 days to get rid of everything and to have the house rented out to a good tenant.

With Ed and I both working full-time, we knew that this would be extremely stressful and we needed to be organized to get this done while searching for a good tenant and getting rid of stuff on a tight deadline.

We picked up a planning calendar at the Dollar Store and started mapping out our plans, budget and target dates.

This would be our master planner; that we could share and refer to, making sure that we stayed on track.

Our first plan of attack was to get the house rented. So, we made a list of next steps:

- ➢ stage house for photos

- ➢ take good pictures of all rooms

- ➢ post free listing on Craig's list

- ➢ screen and interview applicants

- ➢ prepare 1 year renewable lease

We placed a free ad in Craig's list, listing our house for rent.

For those of you who are not familiar with Craig's list (also known as Craigslist[7]), it is one of the best free resources for classifieds ads for selling, buying, and job searching on the internet. There is a Craigslist classified in every major city and country in the world.

Now with anything free you, have to be careful of scammers or criminals as Craigslist is known to attract

---

[7] www.craigslist.org

those types of people. When posting ads, do not list any personal information, or post jewelry that is valuable for sale as you do not want to be a target. In our city, a businessman posted some jewelry for sale and when the buyers came to visit the seller, he was robbed at gun point.

In having the most success with an ad, you have to be specific in all your descriptions to appeal to the right tenant. You need to screen as much as possible so that your time is not wasted. Ask for references and look for inconsistencies and if your intuition says that it is wrong, go with your instincts as they are usually more right than wrong.

It was very important to find a good tenant, as landlord –tenant laws are strict in Ontario where tenants seem to have more rights than the landlords and once you have bad tenants they are difficult to evict.

Bad tenants will drain your time and resources as they know how to get around local laws. Good screening is critical in the long run versus looking at the immediate financial benefit.

We listed our 3 bedroom executive home for lease and posted pictures of the house and all the rooms.

Before listing we researched the rental market on our friend Google[8] to determine how much rent we wanted to charge and had a fixed price in mind and left a little wiggle room for negotiation if a good tenant should come around.

Our second plan was to look at what we needed to get rid of, what we needed to sell, what we needed to keep and what we needed to donate. Ed and I would tackle each room nightly, starting with the kitchen. It worked out well at first, until we started having arguments concerning keeping which items with sentimental value to keep and which to dispose of.

After a week it seemed like the pile of stuff to get rid of was smaller than the pile of what we were going to keep. Sorting together was not going to work because we would not get rid of anything.

We knew that we could not do this alone and decided that we would get an assistant to help us.

---

[8] https://www.google.com/

PENNY SMART

We again used Craigslist to post an ad for an assistant because we figured that with the money that we would receive from selling our stuff, it would pay for his/her wages and we would have some left over.

The ad was placed as follows:

Hands on Assistant – Trustworthy with Driver's License and Vehicle for 2 month assignment- 20 hrs + weekly, cash paid. Work independently to assist owners that are moving with packing boxes, cleaning house, storage runs, raking, dump runs, donation runs, posting items for sale on line, organize garage sales, some heavy lifting, starting ASAP once references are verified. Assignment may extend to additional hours. Email resume and references.

The response was amazing as we received over 20 resumes.

I narrowed my interview to two good candidates. To save on time, I did the interviews first by phone and then by person. I asked the following interview questions by phone:

➢ Have you ever moved and packed a house before?

> ➢ What organization skills do you have?

> ➢ And how would you apply them to assist us?

> ➢ How do you qualify yourself as being trustworthy?

> ➢ What have you done before to be in a position of trust?

> ➢ Have you worked under pressure before to get things done?

It was important to find someone who was trustworthy as they would have access to some of our personal information and would need to sell items on our behalf and collect funds.

Once I met with the two candidates, I made my decision based on the way they responded to the interview questions and my gut instincts.

I truly believe that timing is everything as I was lucky to find the perfect match. The person who was hired to be my assistant was a cute English lady with a wonderful sense of humour who had recently moved

---

to the area, had just completed a large move with her family with packing, sorting and selling and seemed very organized.

This was going to be fun as she was perfect for the job and all of her references had checked out.

Good screening with the right questions will help. When interviewing, let the person do most of the talking and you do most of the listening, as this will help you assess the person and their trustworthiness.

This cute English lady was going to be my right hand, she would learn to understand how I think and be objective in helping me let go of my stuff. Once she signed off on the confidentiality agreement we started the process.

Having a confidentiality agreement in place protects your privacy when you are hiring someone and allowing them to access your information.

A person who is trustworthy will have no problems in signing such an agreement.

If you do a search on line there are many free templates that you can access to develop your own.

RVing the Cool Lifestyle Way

Disappearing in 90 days

We needed to be organized, so we created a list of items.

Initial items to buy to start process:

- ➢ Coil notebook

- ➢ Paper

- ➢ Labels for pricing

- ➢ Duct tape

- ➢ Large Plastic Containers for Sorting

- ➢ Boxes to be used for garage sale

- ➢ Markers

We had a tight deadline to meet, so we used a spiral coil notebook that would be a project management journal for the both of us. I would fill it with "A To Do List" for her to complete in my absence and she would post any questions and enter her hours, so that I could pay her.

In the coil notebook, the headings would be:

Penny Smart

- ➢ Date

- ➢ To Do List

- ➢ Hours worked

- ➢ Accomplished

- ➢ Outstanding Questions

My assistant was to work independently and then we would sit down twice a week to go over priorities and then set the next action steps.

This system worked great as it gave my assistant the independence to work on her own.

We started the sorting process to categorize:

- ➢ What items do we keep?

- ➢ What do we give to family?

- ➢ What do we take with us?

- ➢ What do we get rid of?

- ➢ What we need to sell?

- ➢ What do we donate?

RVing the Cool Lifestyle Way
Disappearing in 90 days

I needed to change my way of thinking, especially about purging and not keeping items that would take up space, which is at a premium now.

We divided our house into the following:

> ➢ Garage right side - items for dumping

> ➢ Garage left side – items to be donated to charity

> ➢ Kitchen Area – items for sale to be priced

> ➢ Dining Room – items to RV

> ➢ Guest Bedroom – items to storage

> ➢ Spare Bedroom – items to give to family

The exercise to get rid of our stuff was very painful as we had accumulated collections of antiques, chinaware, glassware, pottery, artwork that we thought were good investments at the time of purchase and found we were attached to for sentimental reasons.

Penny Smart

Learning to let go was a difficult process, but once we got over the hump it was easy.

You quickly realize that you cannot get the original value back of an item if you are in a hurry to get rid of it.

We wanted to start thinking simple and not have to worry about stuff again.

We did manage to put some valuable items away in storage in the vinyl storage containers that we sealed carefully to prevent any vermin from getting in. We numbered the containers and labelled what the items were on a master record, in case we ever needed to retrieve them again and forgot the contents.

In the garage I did a quick study on the "dispose of pile" and added up how much I paid retail for all of the items, it added up to almost a thousand dollars. It was discouraging to know that was money wasted on buying things that are gadgets and fads and were now being thrown away.

Online classifieds, such as Craigslist[9], Amazon[10], Kijii[11] and Ebay, I found are the best ways to get rid of stuff.

---

[9] http://www.craigslist.org

The quickest way to post items on Craigslist was to use my iPad, or another Smartphone device, to take pictures and post ads through the Craigslist App. This way each ad took less than 3 minutes to write up a description and post a picture as we had many items to post. The only hold up was when our Wi-fi was slow in uploading the picture.

With Craigslist all postings are free, if you are considering using Ebay or Amazon you need to pay listing fees and you should read their policies before listing as they do change from time to time.

We decided to post a majority of the items for sale on free classified sites such as Craigslist as we had less than 70 days left and a tight budget.

 On Craigslist we have found that you have to keep reposting the ad to keep it on top of the lists without paying listing fees.

---

[10] http://www.amazon.com/

[11] http://www.ebayclassifieds.com/

PENNY SMART

With the higher end items, we took them to the local consignment stores for resale. We sorted through all of my business clothes and donated them to a Women's shelter and hospital resale store. It felt good to get rid of items by donating to a charity.

My husband Ed was good at keeping his clothes to a minimal as he didn't need 5 pairs of shoes to match suits and so on like I did. I certainly learned through this exercise of downsizing that you need to minimize. What is the point of having 5 pairs of shoes, when you normally only use two. The other three take up space. I still have more than 5 pairs of shoes, but not as much as I used to have.

We started evaluating the pros of living a simpler, clutter-less life, as we had been seduced into filling empty household space with unnecessary things by clever marketers.

I learned through this process of downsizing to develop a quick checklist whenever I now go shopping.

Shopping Checklist:

> ➢ Do I need it?

➢ Is in my budget?

➢ Will it be clutter?

➢ Why do I need it?

➢ What do I need to get rid of to replace with this purchase?

With only 8 weeks left, we decided setting up garage sales would be the best way to get rid of stuff. It was spring and there was snow on the ground.

We were safe with an enclosed area, if it started snowing.

We started having weekly garage sales and set out the following plan:

➢ Post ad in local paper one week in advance

➢ Highlight a high value item in the ad to draw attention

➢ Make six signs with green neon cardboard sheets

Penny Smart

> ➢ Use "Moving Sale" headline

> ➢ Put signs up the night before the sale in a high traffic area

> ➢ Post signs up where events are happening

We were surprised by how many people would actually come out in the cold weather for a garage sale.

We leveraged the signs by also posting the signs in areas where there were events happening with high traffic. Before having the garage sale, we set out the guidelines so that we would be consistent in price negotiating with bargain seekers.

When you start having garage sales you will find that there are professional dealers that come around looking for bargains and there are also many people who will expect you to give away your items for almost nothing. You will need to be somewhat strict on your pricing.

You do need to put garage sale prices on items if you wish to sell them quickly.

People like to see prices on items, that way you don't lose a sale. I have been to many garage sales where I just walked away as nothing was priced and the owner was engaged in a conversation and I didn't want to interrupt.

For pricing, I use the rule of about 25 to 30% of the original cost. For items such as books, CD's, DVD's I use the range of anywhere from $1.00 to $5.00 which worked perfectly.

Since it was difficult for me to sell and let go of everything, it was best that I was not there and let my assistant handle all the sales.

We developed "Garage Sale Guidelines in my absence," so that everyone was clear with expectations as we had a tight deadline to meet:

- ➤ Establish and put prices on all items before bringing out

- ➤ Put brightly colored items out in front to attract

- ➤ Post moving sale ad on Craigslist the night before

Penny Smart

- ➤ Keep a float box of $25.00 with small change

- ➤ Have content boxes of set price items such as $1.00, $2.00 etc. to put stuff into

- ➤ Keep pen, paper & calculator available

- ➤ Have shopping bags handy

- ➤ If purchasing several items take $2.00 off

- ➤ Contact us if negotiating for more than $30

- ➤ Start at 8am and finish by 2pm on Saturdays

With this process we conducted 6 weekend garage sales and earned over $4,000, while getting rid of unwanted stuff and completing everything in 80 days.

During the last weekend before we were to move out, we still had some stuff left over which we donated to the local church for their annual yard sale. They came and picked everything up, which helped clean out our garage.

We came out ahead and I was able to pay my assistant her earnings plus a bonus and we still had some funds left over.

If you are downsizing such as we did from a 2,000 square home to 370 square feet of RV living space, you can do it by keeping focused with a daily notebook that you can review to ensure you are on track with your goals.

Once we moved, we still had to keep purging to be organized as old habits are hard to get rid of. We would post notes on our mirrors to remind us to

"Keep It Smart, Simple & clean". (KISS)

FIGURE 3 - FRONT INTERIOR OF AN RV

ART OF BECOMING MOBILE

"That's been one of my mantras — focus and simplicity. Simple can be harder than complex: You have to work hard to get your thinking clean to make it simple. But it's worth it in the end because once you get there, you can move mountains."
-Steve Jobs

After the tight time frame of constant, non-stop downsizing, there was the mental aspect of getting accustomed to living in small quarters on wheels as this was no longer part-time RV living but now full-time RV living.

We were living in less than 25% of our original quarters and space was at a premium with our closets filled to capacity.

RVing the Cool Lifestyle Way
Art of Becoming Mobile

With our seasonal business in operation, we did not have much time to think about it as we worked hard and crashed at night in the RV, as if it was just sleeping quarters.

But when we did think about it, it was a sad feeling of leaving our spacious waterfront home of 25 years to move down to an one room area of less than 500 square feet with a divider separating the bedroom and living room/dining area.

There is an art to becoming mobile as it is a departure from what we were normally accustomed to.

Namely, you really need to get along as friends as in a small space as there is no escaping to a private area if there are disagreements, although you could still have a bit of space by drawing the divider, staying in the washroom or having one person leave. The main rule is to get along. Life is too short and valuable to have bad feelings and disagreements, so stay happy as much as possible.

My biggest adjustment was going from the washroom ensuite with a spa to a small shared washroom space that was smaller than my original home closet with only a shower. I had enjoyed spreading my makeup palettes and face creams on my vanity, but now had only the kitchen table and a small makeup bag.

I had to learn to put things away as it can get messy quickly in a small space. Instead of having two or three of everything, you learn not to buy more than you need as you don't have any space for storage as everything is styled for being compact.

I also missed my weekly bubble baths and as an alternative we always seek resorts that have swimming pools and hot-tubs for that weekly fix.

You also need to manage shared washroom space, as men are usually in the washroom longer because they use it for their thinking and get away time.

Since there was no privacy if the television was on, I invested in a pair of noise control headsets which enabled me to continue to communicate, work and listen to music without hearing outside interference.

Looking for Wi-Fi in local RV parks was important and it was interesting to note that in Canada, not all areas are Wi-Fi ready with good receiving towers. So, a lot of research needs to be done first before staying in any

RV park. There is a free app called WIFI[12] finder that can assist you in finding Wi-Fi.

The other was to be organized with paperwork because with our limited space, there was no room for large filing cabinets and a desk as I was accustomed to in my own private office.

It was a good feeling though to get rid of all my paperwork at the house, which was a huge job in itself, and to save everything electronically.

We evaluated the pros and cons, did we want mortgaged luxury and paying high expenses or an affordable lifestyle that we would enjoy for the next 15 years while we still have our health and are able to travel and have fun?

The pros of living simple, such as being able to clean house in less than an hour and living south during the winter, certainly outweighed the any of the cons.

---

[12] https://itunes.apple.com/us/app/wi-fi-finder/id300708497?mt=8

PENNY SMART

Careful planning needed to be done as we were moving to a more mobile lifestyle and we needed a checklist to ensure that we did not miss anything if we did start a life of mobile living.

ART OF BEING MOBILE CHECKLIST:

- ✓ Passports are up to date

- ✓ Ensure Wills are in order

- ✓ Power of Attorney –Financial is in place for your absence

- ✓ Power of Attorney –Health Care in place

- ✓ Life insurance documents in order

- ✓ Photocopy all important documents, scan and save on a USB stick or password protected Cloud space.

- ✓ If bringing pets, bring papers & vaccination proof

- ✓ Get adequate out of country travel insurance

- ✓ Check vehicle insurance is up to date and okay for out of country travel

---

- ✓ Credit card and debit card that can be used in USA & Canada

- ✓ Carry enough cash to last a few days, as you can always do a cash back at large grocery and department stores from your debit card

- ✓ Have RV auto coverage such as CAA or AAA

- ✓ Map out destination and stops before leaving- have on a paper format

- ✓ Research destination for Wi-Fi access

- ✓ Have diary & budget planner

- ✓ Bring up to date medical records

Our family and friends would ask how can you do that?

And I would reply, it is a lifestyle change that is really no different than people who want to live on their boat or yacht all year round, it is our chance for adventure. You only live life once.

PENNY SMART

Once your children leave you are free to do just about anything and I would laugh saying that this is the 21ˢᵗ century lifestyle, upscale simple gypsy living with bells and whistles and technology at your fingertips. It is our dream life.

Once you have gotten rid of all the accumulated stuff that you didn't need, you realize what you spent on unneeded items could have been put away as additional funds to help sustain your lifestyle in the upcoming mature years.

It's funny how we back track on what we should have done right, but now it is time to move forward.

 It initially gave me a lot of grief to part with items that I thought I was emotionally attached to, yet once they were gone, I didn't think about them until someone else mentioned them.

We knew in advance that the cycle of living as a full-timer would only last 10 to 15 years at the most.

We also realized that living in an RV all year round in northern parts of America such as in Canada was not possible as RVs are not made for this, with the chance of pipes freezing once temperatures go below zero.

RVing the Cool Lifestyle Way

Art of Becoming Mobile

If you live in a cold climate, yet wish to become a full-time RVer then you must travel to a hotter climate in the winter.

This lifestyle would work perfectly for as we work in the summer in our seasonal business and in the winter travel to the southern states to be in a warm climate.

ORGANIZING BASICS

"Yesterday is history, tomorrow is a mystery, today is a gift of God, which is why we call it the present."
— Bil Keane

The basics of being organized in anything is to Keep It Simple and Smart (KISS) and to use no more than three to five categories, anything more than that makes it difficult to remember.

There are five core elements to being organized while by being mobile for full-timer RVers. They are:

1. Banking

2. Correspondence (Mail & Email)

3. Document Management

4. Phone

5. Internet Wi-Fi Access

You only need to think of these five areas so that you are not overwhelmed. Organize your computer and smartphone same way as there is a lot of noise with technology.

BANKING

"Our greatest glory is not in never falling, but in rising every time we fall."
— Confucius

For managing your money and paying your bills on time, it is best have a bank account setup in your home country base with online banking access.

Having online banking can allow you to monitor your balances on a daily basis, help detect fraudulent incidents and help you budget. You are able to pay bills, transfer and receive funds almost instantly with online banking.

It is quite straight forward to do this with any national bank and most have apps that can be downloaded on your smartphone so that you can monitor your account daily or weekly.

It is best to deal with a national bank that has a cross border presence as this is handy for setting up a new banking relationship with their sister branches in the country that you are staying in.

Setting up a bank account:

- ✓ Make an appointment first, ask about requirements

- ✓ Bring 2 pieces of Government issued ID, passport and Driver's License

- ✓ Minimum cash deposit of $100[13]

- ✓ Obtain a debit card

- ✓ Arrange to have electronic bank statements emailed to you.

To pay bills online, in travel mode, do one of the following:

- ✓ Pay bills online directly

---

[13] Varies with each bank

PENNY SMART

- ✓ Give authorization to the Biller

- ✓ Preauthorize monthly set payments and
  pay the difference the following month

- ✓ Set up one-time payment transfers

Receiving Payments while in Travel Mode:

- ✓ Make advance arrangements with bank to
  assist with deposits that can be mailed to
  them directly for deposit

- ✓ Arrange for them to send you internet bank
  transfer by email

- ✓ Arrange for direct deposit for payments for
  Government and Work related income

If you are considering full-time RVing, it will save you money to have two separate bank accounts starting with one where you normally reside and file your taxes with, and the other one in the country that you are living part-time in.

It will help you establish cross border credit with a banking relationship and you can get additional savings when shopping online as some retailers and services only accept USD or CDN based debit/visa cards.

Other benefits include applying for loans and other financial services that you won't qualify for unless you have US-based accounts. You can also deposit US issued cheques into a US-based account which is normally cleared quicker.

If you have an existing relationship with a bank in your home country explore if they have an international presence, which makes it easier to do money transfers and obtain funds between countries.

If you already have a US account with a Canadian bank, it should be noted that they are not connected, as both countries have different regulations and banking systems.

While you can apply at your home bank before crossing the border, there may be additional fees involved and it is not as straight forward as visiting the bank directly in the country that you are living in.

PENNY SMART

Visit the US bank branch in-person, the best way to set up a bank account is by face-to-face personal meeting.

The best banking experience that I have heard from others in dealing across the border is with TD bank for both personal and business matters.

If you maintain a minimal monthly balance there are no fees charged. Once you set up a bank account, you are issued a debit card to do US-based transactions and can access your account anytime through the internet.

Here are three National Canadian equivalents to the US banks & vice versa.

Banking

Canadian Bank   Equals   US Bank

TD Canada Trust Bank	=	TD Bank
Bank of Montreal	=	BMO Harris Bank
Royal Bank (RBC)	=	PNC Bank

In order to set up a US bank account you need to have a physical address in the US, which can be a relative's address or a mail forwarding address. It cannot be a post office box.

US-BASED CREDIT CARDS

"Be yourself; everyone else is already taken."
— Oscar Wilde

By setting up a credit card in the USA or Canada, it allows you to establish a credit history in a different country and qualify for cash rebates, points and good discounts with your visa card. Some online retailers will only process an order that has a credit card with a US-based address that is automatically verified. Once you have a US based credit card it can open doors for many other discount saving opportunities as there are many stores that offer rebates.

There are two ways of getting a US-based credit card; the first way is to apply for a credit card where you have set up the new account with your bank branch in the US. It may be difficult without having a social security number and credit card history.

You are most likely going to get credit approval if you have a pre-existing relationship with your Canadian bank, as a Canadian credit report will be done through the Canadian bank and information given to the US bank for the approval process. Remember that systems between the US and Canadian banks are not connected.

The other is a deposit on hold with $500.00. You can set up a credit card with the $500.00 on hold as security for 2 years, though there will be a small fee to do this. The other alternative is the prepaid Visa cards, which are the most expensive and time consuming to use.

ATM and Debit Cards:

Once you are issued a debit card, you are free to use it anywhere where there is a debit machine. You can also withdraw funds anywhere there is a debit ATM (Automatic Teller Machine). Though be careful of using ATM machines that are in unknown places, as there have been recent incidents of skimming, where imprints of the card and PIN are taken and then your account is emptied. Also using ATMs like this can cost

PENNY SMART

you up to $5.00 per transaction with a bank's charge and the ATM's host charge. If you use a Canadian-based debit card in the US, there are also associated fees for the use. I have found the best way to use debit cards is through grocery stores or large shopping stores that offer cash back when you pay for items by debit.

MAIL FORWARDING

"If I had a flower for every time I thought of you...I could walk through my garden forever."
— Alfred Tennyson

Mail forwarding addresses serve two purposes, for banking as you cannot open a bank account without a physical address and also for redirecting mail to your location as you are travelling.

In order to open a bank account, you need to have a physical address nearby where you will be opening the account.

There are hundreds of mail forwarding services that will provide a virtual address which can serve as your

Penny Smart

permanent address if you are not stationary a period of time.

You will need to do a keyword search with my good friend Google to find one, using the keyword "Mail Forwarding Address." The fee for this service ranges from $10.00 a month to $50.00 month. A majority of the mail forwarding services will charge you a monthly base fee and then additional fees for forwarding the mail which can be delivered within 48 hours to your location. Make sure you check out reviews to see if you are dealing with a reputable one.

DOCUMENT MANAGEMENT

"If you tell the truth, you don't have to remember anything."
— Mark Twain

Once you understand the art of becoming mobile you need to be organized so that you manage your mail, bill payments, banking and communication while you are travelling. You need to simplify your filing to only five categories where you save documents.

You will need to be able to access documents and information when you need to, you do not need to be a filing cabinet on wheels.

PENNY SMART

Personally, I have done banking, signed contracts, negotiated and closed deals using the internet and my smartphone.

There are two components of being organized, first managing your documents and pictures in a paper form and then managing them electronically, saving and organizing them on a Cloud in the same format so that they are accessible at any time.

You may choose to just manage paper-wise, but more companies and banks are starting to think green and save on resources by sending out bills electronically. It is useful to know how to manage your documents by naming and tagging them so that they are easily located if you save them electronically or on a Cloud.

The biggest time waster is trying to locate something. The more time you spend setting up a proper system, the more ahead you will be in the long run.

Here is an example of the system that works for us. You only need to set up master folders in only five categories. You need to think only in five, as this is also how you will manage your smartphone and have it set up the same way, from there you can set up subcategories with only five per category, otherwise you will spend hours trying to find saved files that are not filed properly.

KISS Virtual file Management					
File Naming	Define Year = YYYY	Month= MM	Day =DD	Simple File Name =XXXXX	Example = 2013.03.12.Phone
MASTER FOLDER NAMES	Folder NAME	Folder Name	Folder Name	Folder Name	Folder Name
Personal File Folders	TO DO	Banking	Correspondence	Income	Expenses
Business File Folders	TO DO	Banking	Correspondence	Customers	Suppliers
Media	PLAY	HOME	WORK	Keep file naming consistent	

Personal Home File Virtual Setup:

    A. To Do

    B. Banking

    C. Correspondence

    D. Income

E. Expenses

When filing electronic files, you need to setup master file folders by pre-naming them with letters, which will help it sort the files in the order that you want. Once you categorize documents and tag them by date and name they are easily sorted in the master files. As an example you would save your phone bill document once as 2013.03.12_phone, then next one would be 2013.04.12_phone, it would be automatically sorted in sequence and easy to locate, if you do a search for the word "phone".

Paper file folders can also be set up in the same way, for income tax purposes, I paper clip all the expenses together such as phone bills, utilities, etc. I use a small filing box and once the year is completed and handed over to the accountant and scanned virtually and saved on USB stick or on a cloud, they can be shredded to save you space.

Significant advances have been made also in cloud technology, which means you can save information on a cloud and access it anytime or anywhere in the world securely. There are free cloud services that are available on the internet or through an app with Microsoft called Skydrive[xvi] or Google called G-Drive[xvii] where you can save your documents and pictures on a cloud. The best one I have found is a paid service called <u>Dropbox</u>[xviii], which is initially free with limited space.

EMAIL SETUP

"Every child is an artist. The problem is how to remain an artist once he grows up."
— Pablo Picasso

There are several free email services that are available, such as Yahoo, Aol, Hotmail, Google and many more. The top two email services that I use are Gmail and Hotmail, the reason being that they have good security, spam filters, free cloud space and free office applications such as word processing and spreadsheets along with other tools that can help with being mobile and organized.

You will need to set one up for your electronic mail. I use three email addresses; one for specific tasks, one for online shopping and registering to different sites online, and the other just for personal use. The shopping email gets flooded with junk mail, so I only check it once a week.

To be organized you can register the same name with all three services if you want to have more than one email with the same user name. For example, using the name "anyone" at all three services, giving you the following three emails anyone@gmail.com, anyone@yahoo.com, anyone@hotmail.com. These email addresses can also be forwarded to your main email address if you like.

Here are some tips:

➢ When registering for an email address, do it at the privacy of your home on your smartphone and not in a public area such as a library or anywhere there is public Wi-Fi unless it is secure.

➢ Do not use your address as a password or something simple that hackers can figure out.

➢ Write your password down and keep in a safe place, do not share with anyone.

> ➢ Set up your folders the same way as in the file management section.

> ➢ When emails come in you can set up rules or labels so that they are categorized right away and just need to be archived when you finish reading them.

When signing up for email public services, I never give my real date of birth due to identify theft. However, if you decide to do this, you must remember what you have used in case you need to retrieve your password as that may be one of the security questions.

From your computer, go to the following and follow their instructions to set up an email account:

Setting up a Gmail account:

> ➢ https://mail.google.com

Setting up a Yahoo account:

> ➢ http://www.yahoo.com/

Setting up a Hotmail account:

> ➢ https://login.live.com

___

There are also apps available for Gmail, Yahoo and Hotmail, that you can download and sign up.

PENNY SMART

PHONE PLANS TO SAVE

"Imperfection is beauty, madness is genius and it's better to be absolutely ridiculous than absolutely boring."
— Marilyn Monroe

If you travelling you want to avoid paying for roaming charges and long distance calls ,which can be extremely high when crossing over from one country to another. As soon as you cross over the border, it is wise to turn your phone off and purchase a prepaid plan in the country that you are in.

Prepaid plans are rapidly becoming the best type of phone plans to use as they have no long-term commitment or contracts, which can save you a lot of money. You pay for services you need by the month in advance from $15.00 to $60.00 and refill again for the next month. The majority of these plans have the same features as long term plans with internet access and international calling features along with other options.

With some of these prepaid plans, you may need to purchase a phone supplied by the carrier which will also include a phone number that may not be transferrable if you decide not to continue with the plan and your phone number may be assigned to someone else.

Many people are finding prepaid plans to be a cost-effective solution to their communication needs. Many parents give these type of phones to their children to limit their usage and because it is affordable and has no long-term commitment.

If you are locked into a phone plan, you will need to wait until your contract is completed to do this otherwise you will have early termination fees.

By purchasing a phone outright, you can save hundreds of dollars through prepaid plans.

PENNY SMART

When purchasing a phone long-term plan through a specific plan carrier, it is usually discounted and SIM locked.

An unlocked phone means that it can be used by a majority of the carriers and you just need a specific SIM card to be inserted in the phone to access their cellular networks.

Phone carriers put SIM locks on the phone to provide discounted phones so that you commit to a long-term contract and cannot use another carrier during the term; however once you terminate your contract most phones can be unlocked with a code.

Unlocked phones can be purchased at most major department stores that carry cellular phones or online from reputable sellers at Amazon or Ebay, Best Buy and others.

There are many known US carriers such as Virgin, Mobile T, Metro PCS that offer prepaid plans, I have found three good suppliers that don't have the huge marketing budgets to advertise but have excellent reviews and plans:

1) Consumer Cellular [xix](USA) is rated highly by consumers on the ATT network. They offer

the lowest cost monthly plans from $10.00 per month to $50.00 per month.

2) SIMple Mobile ˣˣ(USA) sells SIM cards that work on T-Mobile's network at SIMple Mobile's own rates from $30 to $50 month with one time activation fee, it offers internet & international coverage, 4 G, texting and works well on unlocked phones and iPhones.

3) H2O Wireless ˣˣⁱ(USA) runs on AT&T's national GSM network, and offers plans by the month, day, or minute. Minute plans are available in $10, $20, $30, and $100 packages, which include 5-cent voice minutes and text messages, as well as 30 cents per MB for data.

In Canada competitive phone services with prepaid plans has been slow coming however, in order to attract the student marketplace, the coverage for

PENNY SMART

prepaid plans is expanding. Here are two carriers that offer these plans in Canada:

1) Koodo Mobile[xxii] (CDN) runs on Telus national CDMA network, and offers low cost plans available as low as $20 per month packages and has national coverage.

2) Virgin Mobile [xxiii](CDN) runs on Bell Mobility CDMA network, and offers low cost plans available as low as $20 to $35.00 per month packages and has national coverage.

How Does Wi-Fi Work?

A wonderful fact to reflect upon, that every human creature is constituted to be that profound secret and mystery to every other."
— Charles Dickens

Wi-Fi is different than using a cellular networks, it uses an air network and is used by millions of computer users, especially those who are RV travellers. With Wi-Fi, outgoing data is translated into a radio signal and transmitted using an antenna. This signal is encrypted so only a device that can decrypt its code will be able to analyze the signal.

PENNY SMART

You will see free Wi-Fi hotspots everywhere: in coffee shops like Starbucks, MacDonald's, libraries and in many other advertised public areas, even at public beaches. There is an app that will help you find free Wi-Fi services in any location where you are near.

Generally people feel comfortable in opening their smartphones and laptops to access the free airtime without even thinking.

Wi-Fi uses radio waves to communicate the same way a radio or television works, only it operates both ways. One should be warned that transmitting any information over Wi-Fi is not secure and many identities have been stolen using these services.

I would not recommend accessing any banking information over a public Wi-Fi area or accessing confidential documents without any security in place. Wi-Fi in public areas is good for making phone calls through VOIP such as Skype and other phone services, emails, downloading, doing research, texting and other tasks that do not contain sensitive materials.

While travelling and if you need to create your own hot spot, you can purchase a WiFi enabled smart phone that will allow you to tether so that your computer can access the internet anytime. You can purchase a personal Mi-Fi Mobile Hot Spot from any of the major technology retail outlets which range from $129 and load up with a refill card. I personally have used Virgin's Mi-Fi, which worked well when we needed email and internet to connect our computer and phones to use VOIP access on the go. These personal hotspots are not good for streaming videos as you are allotted a limited amount of bandwidth. However, you can always top off with refills if you need more bandwidth during the month.

Penny Smart

Using Wi-Fi to save $$

"On savings: A dollar here, a dollar there. Over time, it adds up to two dollars. "
— Jarod Kintz

We learned the hard way as we travelled across the border and used our Canadian cell phone carrier for answering emails, doing web searches and phone calls when we got a hefty phone bill after we came home for roaming and long distance charges that was just as much as our vacation.

Had we used Wi-Fi instead of our cell phone, we could have saved ourselves the roaming charges. Wi-Fi is a different technology than using cell phones, which use cellular networks and towers; Wi-Fi uses a radio wave and is connected to the internet.

RVing the Cool Lifestyle Way

Using Wi-Fi to Save $$

You will see phones that say Wi-Fi enabled, which means that if you have Wi-Fi turned on your cellular it will access the Wi-Fi air network instead of the cellular networks which can save you money on emails, texting, surfing and downloading.

An indicator on your smart phone will show you whether or not you are in a Wi-Fi area if you have a WIFI enabled phone.

VOIP PHONES

What you fear most will determine whether you merely save for the future or give for the future."
— Andy Stanley

When using Wi-Fi, we use a VOIP (Voice Over the Internet Protocol) phone for our personal and business calls. This means we get phone calls over the internet versus on a phone line which can save you hundreds of dollars on your phone bill.

Now for this to work properly, you need good internet service and a cable hookup that can be connected to a internet router directly.

We have saved thousands of dollars using this method for our business versus a regular phone line as VOIP technology is about half of the cost. You can use

RVing the Cool Lifestyle Way
VOIP Phones

VOIP for personal or business use. Occasionally you will get low signals but 95% of time, it has been good.

The main advantage of VOIP is that you can take your number anywhere with you as long as there is a direct internet connection.

For our business we take our phone with us and connect it to the internet when we arrive at our destination. When someone calls our number in Canada, we can answer it in Florida and our business or home number in Canada shows up on their phone display which is so cool.

Penny Smart

FREE INTERNET PHONES

"This above all: to thine own self be true, And it must follow, as the night the day, Thou canst not then be false to any man."
— William Shakesphere, Hamlet

Skype (www.skype.com) ˣˣⁱᵛis the internet phone service owned by Microsoft that allows you to connect other Skype users across the world for free. For about $40.00 per year, you can get a US based phone number that can be used on your smartphone.

Pinger (www.pinger.com)ˣˣᵛ is an app that offers free phone and texting for 60 minutes.

INTERNET TV

"The habit of being happy enables one to be freed, largely freed, from domination of outward conditions."
— Robert Louis Stevenson

With bandwidth becoming available at lower cost, online streaming is very popular and allows you to access movies the same way you would if you walked into a video store to rent a DVD, only it is in the comfort of your RV, no more gas wasted travelling and space wasted storing movies. You just click and you can have access to thousands of movies and TV shows which, for a very low cost, which are streamed onto your computer or smart phone device.

Netflix[xxvi], is the most established company that offers the biggest selection of movies and only costs $8.00 a month. The newest DVD releases will be mailed to you as they have a limited selection of new releases in downloads. You can try the service for free for 30 days. There are additional accessories that you can purchase so that you may also stream onto your TV or big screen.

Hulu and Hulu Plus [xxvii] is only available in the US and provides the biggest variety of TV shows online, showing 24 hours after they are aired on TV. They teamed up with the national TV networks to provide this service and offer a free trial for a week and monthly subscriptions for $8.00.

SMARTPHONES

"Everything you can imagine is real."
— Pablo Picasso

Smartphones were not built for just taking calls, emails or playing games. These phones were designed for something greater, hence the terminology "Smartphone." They are used globally around the world, including third world countries for business and resources.

While your smartphone will already come with some built in Apps that can assist you with being productive, such as a camera, video maker, note taking, calendars, weather, search engines and more, there are thousands of Apps that can be purchased directly from your phone at the App store. Whether you have an iPhone, Android or other brand, they will all come with basic starter apps that are very cool.

Figure 4 Apple iPhone

Can it Help me?

Every single time you help somebody stand up you are helping humanity rise."
— Steve Maraboli

A smartphone can instantly help an RVer become really cool and smart. It is a powerful tool that has just as many features as your laptop, except it is portable and can save you a lot of time in performing tasks.

With a one finger touch while in-line waiting or relaxing somewhere, an RVer can have access to variety of resources quickly that can make their life a whole lot easier.

PENNY SMART

Smartphones are being integrated more into our daily lives, just think back to when ATMs started becoming a normal way of banking.

You can set up notifications on your smartphone when you are shopping for something and if it becomes available, it will notify you.

All you need to do is think about is a non-physical task that you need done and a smartphone will help you accomplish that. Think of it as personal helper that does not talk back and just performs at your command.

From making phone calls, to keeping your calendar and address book organized, banking, watching a favorite show, playing your music, giving you driving or walking directions, taking pictures, checking your emails, texting, education, translations, dictation and doing countless other things, a smartphone or tablet can actually save you thousands of dollars if you set it up properly.

Unlike many traditional cell phones, smartphones allow individual users to install, configure and run applications of their choosing.

RVing the Cool Lifestyle Way

Can it Help me?

The smartphone can be configured to your personal liking and any type of task management; it offers the ability to conform the device to your particular way of doing email that can be synced across your computer and phone so that both have the same information at the same time, saving you time and resources. The key is spending the time to set it up properly otherwise you lose valuable time and resources to get it correctly done.

Figure 5-face plate from Android

Smartphones are made simple so the learning curve is minimal; if a 4 year old can figure it out so can you.

PENNY SMART

We have been taught to do things the complicated way through manuals and programs, but smartphones are all visual icon driven. Look at the illustration on icons from the previous page that display on a smartphone as as if they are self-explanatory. Remember smartphones are devices that are supposed to make your life simple with a fingertip touch.

SETTING UP TO ASSIST

"Insanity is doing the same thing, over and over again, but expecting different results."
—Albert Einstein

The must have apps that will help you with being efficient should always be on your main screen. To keep it simple, your main page will consist of the same five categories that you have on your desktop, while apps may not say the same description, they are the main categories that will help you manage and organize your life and should always be on your main screen with the other general interest apps used to assist you.

PENNY SMART

1. To Do (Calendar& Notes App)

2. Banking (Banking App)

3. Correspondence (Email & Phone)

4. Income (Financial App)

5. Expense (Financial App)

Apps is the short abbreviation for the name applications, there many apps that are free or offered at a low price, the average being $.99 to $9.99.

There are several ways to get an app, you can download from a site, through a QR code, someone sends you a link or you can download from the APP Store.

The store to purchase apps will always be on your Iphone and will have the name App Store.

To get apps for an iPhone you need to register for an account and you can purchase iTunes cards at department stores in various denominations to place on your account and refill when low or just use your credit card.

Most apps are now made for both iPhone and Android, however, you will still find apps that been developed only for iPhone users in the store and vice versa.

To get an app just do a name search of something that you are looking for by keyword in the store, the same as hunting for something Google and a whole list of apps will appear that have been rated by popularity from other users that will have comments posted with a price or they may be free.

You can buy just about any app that mirrors or functions like a pricey desktop software program. The reason the pricing is so low, is that developers are depending on volume from a worldwide audience rather just local markets. The programing of apps is also a lot easier than computer programming. You can do a search on YouTube and watch teens demonstrate how they show off on how to make an app.

Some apps just provide interfaces to access the higher end software programs that are available over the internet.

There are hundreds of thousand apps out in the worldwide marketplace. Some developers just cater to a geographical area and may not be available for download with an out of country account, as an

PENNY SMART

example there is the Canadian and US Apple app store which are two separate entities, so if you purchase a iTunes card in the USA, it may not work if your account and smart phone store is registered in Canada.

I personally have registered for the US marketplace as I find that there is a better variety of apps to select from. You can have two accounts but it really gets complicated.

If you are looking at banking apps for cross border, it's best to download an app directly from institution's site rather than through the app store to avoid problems.

Apps are priced low and once you purchase an app, there are no refunds however you can post a review if you do not like the app and its functionality.

Almost anything that you can access through the internet, you will be able to do through a smartphone to make your life easy as apps are deployed with a touch of your finger.

FIGURE 6 - PENNY SMART WORKING REMOTELY IN RV

Penny Smart

RVer Apps

"If I'm an advocate for anything, it's to move. As far as you can, as much as you can. Across the ocean, or simply across the river. The extent to which you can walk in someone else's shoes or at least eat their food, it's a plus for everybody. Open your mind, get up off the couch, move."
— Anthony Bourdain

Allstays[xxviii] is a smartphone app that an RVer should not be without, it identifies all campgrounds their facilities, shopping locations for RVers, highway clearance heights, dump stations, Wal-Mart plazas that allow free overnight parking, rest stops and Travel Plaza Stops through a smartphone if you are travelling across North America.

RVing the Cool Lifestyle Way

RVer Apps

<u>Cheap Gas</u>[xxix] this app is great for finding the best price for gas while you are travelling.

<u>FlipBoard</u>[xxx] this app is great for customizing news from your hometown and social media all under one application.

<u>TuneIn Radio</u>[xxxi] this app allows you to tune into any radio station around the world.

<u>TV Towers USA</u>[xxxii] this app will help you find TV towers in the local area for setting up satellite dishes and antennas.

<u>WeatherBug</u>[xxxiii] this app is great for weather, news and can be viewed on desktop as well as all mobile devices.

<u>Walmart</u>[xxxiv] this app has all information for sales and a location finder for all Wal-Marts. You can send your photos for printing directly on this app.

<u>Wifi Finder</u>[xxxv] this app will help you find free WIFI in any area.

Sex & Romance in an RV

"Sex is emotion in motion"
-Mae West

In your RV travels you may come across a beautiful sunset or breathtaking view and want to capture that magic moment. What a nice time to find a secluded spot and crack open that bottle of wine that you have been saving for that romantic time together. If you are travelling around in an RV and suddenly have the urge to have a bit of sexy fun, you are set with an instant hotel room that is ready at a push of a button.

Being in an RV is very intimate and romantic if you want it to be: you don't need a fireplace, just close the curtains and windows and your privacy is all set for those sexy moments as no one will bother you if you appear closed up with your shades drawn in a RV resort. Don't worry about making a little noise, as life is about enjoying the natural pleasures that don't cost you anything. A healthy sex life will certainly keep you young and active.

You can create a moment by starting with some romantic music. One cool free app that plays romantic music from around the world is one called Valentine Radio[xxxvi] which I enjoy. There are several apps that can also spice up your sex life, one is called the Kamsutra [xxxvii]app that provides over 100 sensual positions and it can boost your experience while playing relaxing music in the background. If you have read the book 50 Shades of Grey, there is a sex game app called 50 Shades of Grey [xxxviii]that is the perfect companion for the book. There are many other fun sex apps that are available through the app store which you can use as the starting point for a pleasurable experience with your a partner or to increase your knowledge base on everything you wanted to know about sex.

QR Codes Explained

"Learn from yesterday, live for today, hope for tomorrow. The important thing is to not stop questioning."
— Albert Einstein

QR code is a two-dimensional barcode as shown in the above example, is used by organizations worldwide. If you are wondering what QR means, the letters stand for Quick Response because of the codes quick readability.   QR codes are similar to the standard barcodes that you usually see in retail items found in malls or grocery stores. When scanned by an appropriate scanner or a mobile device, it can trigger a number of functions such as sending an SMS, launching a website, viewing Google maps, accessing a coupon and even downloading a file.

Since smartphone usage is on the rise, more and more businesses will be utilizing QR codes for marketing promotions, so have some fun and start scanning wherever you see a QR code.

SOCIAL MEDIA

"A friend is one that knows you as you are,
understands where you have been, accepts what you
have become, and still, gently allows you to grow."
— William Shakespeare

You have most likely heard about Facebook, Twitter, LinkedIn and other social media networks, perhaps you have used them to search for friends or connect with your children. More businesses and general communication is being done these days through this type of media. If you do post anything, just be aware that it will not be as private as they claim it will be.

On Facebook, there are currently over 800 million users which use the application to connect with friends, family, business and social acquaintances to provide social information, news, updates and other personal information. There are privacy settings that can be setup, however whatever you post will always be retained on the internet as it is never private.

RVing the Cool Lifestyle Way

Social Media

Social Networking – Sites such as Twitter and Facebook make it easy for mobile users to receive messages and notifications from fans, followers and those in the know. One click of your button on your Smartphone, and you can read the latest Tweets (which are social messages which contain no more than 160 characters). You can send Tweets and Facebook messages as well as receive them. Apps such as TweetDeck & HootSuite make managing social networks easy, no matter where you are.

Social Bookmarking – You can also store, access and share links easily, right from your smartphone. No more trying to remember links, or scribbling them down while you're out and about.

Digital Media – Mobile devices make it easy for you to utilize audio and video to help you remember things and capture a moment. If you do a video on your smart phone, YouTube is already mobile-ready – all you have to do is upload your video, and let your subscribers know about the link (via text message, email, Tweeting, or posting on your Facebook account).

FIGURE 7 - WIFI CAN BE USED ANYWHERE

MONEY SAVING APPS

Forecasts may tell you a great deal about the forecaster; they tell you nothing about the future."
— Warren Buffet

Using money-saving mobile applications is a very smart way to save your hard-earned money! Here are just some of the few of the best money-saving apps that are available. It is possible to save thousands of dollars just by downloading these from the App store.

PRICE COMPARISON APPS

Price comparison apps let you compare prices from various retailers. Instead of checking each store for prices, you can do it using your mobile phone. Amazon's Price Check[xxxix] is a wonderful price comparison mobile app. Red Laser[xl] by eBay is another great choice. Aside from getting the new prices, you can also look at product descriptions and reviews. With these apps, you don't only save money but your precious time as well.

You can also look for mobile applications of your favorite stores. If you love shopping at the Gap, look for a Gap mobile app. This way, you will receive special discounts and deals that other shoppers won't get.

SHOPPING LIST APPS

Shopping lists can help you save money. Creating a list before heading to the grocery store will eliminate impulse buys. Without a list, it would be so easy to fill-up the cart with unnecessary things. Aside from this, it will help you remember everything you need to buy. You do not have to go back to the supermarket to be tempted with unneeded purchases again. This is where the shopping list apps can help you. An app called Grocery iQ[xli] is a shopping list app which helps organize your list by brand or aisle. It is superior to your normal paper shopping list because there is a sync option which prevents multiple purchases from different members of the family.

RVing the Cool Lifestyle Way

Money Saving Apps

COUPON APPS

Using coupons can save you more money that you have ever expected. Mobile coupon apps will save you the trouble of finding, printing and clipping coupons. All you have to do is download the app and you are good to go! One of the most popular group buying sites, Groupon,[xlii] has a free mobile app. Their app will help you find discounts for shops, restaurant and other products and services. Although they do not offer a lot of deals, you will be sure to see one that you want.

PERSONAL FINANCE APPS

Forget your spreadsheets and calculators! You can stop crunching numbers every night just to make sure your books are balanced. There are many personal finance apps that can help you easily manage your finances anywhere. There are many apps there under this category. However, most are paid apps. Mint[xliii] stands out from the rest because it is free. It doesn't mean that it is not up to par with the paid ones. In fact, it was among the 50 best iPhone apps this year. You can use it for budgeting, expense tracking and

---

analyzing spending habits. It connects directly to your bank account and even notifies you of suspicious transactions.

In this economy, we all should look for ways to stretch our budgets a little bit. There are a lot more apps out there that can help you save more. Take time to look at the other apps – who knows what you will discover! The important thing is to get the apps which are appropriate for your needs.

LOOKING FOR WORK

Our lives are defined by opportunities, even the ones we miss."

— Eric Roth

There are various resources and apps that can be very helpful in assisting you to find work, so that you don't have to physically go anywhere and it can be done quickly through your smartphone with very little effort and at your leisure.

Penny Smart

With job finding apps, you can post your resume online and potential employers will look at your skills and contact you.

With notification settings you can set up the apps to advise you of particular jobs that may be in the area that you are seeking. These apps are very handy as they can locate by postal code and search for the type of work that you are looking for.

The best place to find work is using the app Craigslist Mobile[xliv] you select by job category and location. Other useful apps are Job Aware[xlv], Job Search [xlvi] and Indeed.[xlvii]

Full-time RVers use a site called Workamper[xlviii] which has job postings that combine camping and working at the campground and various RV resort sites.

If you enjoy working on computers and like working virtually on a freelance contract basis, there is Guru[xlix] and Elance[l] where you can bid on jobs that are posted.

BECOMING SMARTER

"Live as if you were to die tomorrow. Learn as if you were to live forever."
— Mahatma Gandhi

While travelling, it can be easy to become restless with not having resources available to keep your mind active and up to date. Perhaps you wanted to get the degree that you always dreamed of or learn a new subject matter. While you can always look up a subject matter on YouTube and watch a video or two, there are countless free education resources that are available where you can get a certificate for no cost that are extremely high end. This is a new trending movement called massive open online courses known as MOOC, which has Time Magazine forecasting that education may be free in the next 10 years.

The top universities in North America are offering free online courses through the site called www.coursera.org.[li]

This site which offers free Harvard based Courses is called www.edx.org.[lii]

Another is free education site that offers over 625 free online courses from leading universities and many other free resources is called www.Openculture.com.[liii]

If you enjoy lectures and learning, talks and interesting topics a good site is www.ted.com.[liv]

FREE E-BOOKS

Here is a list of the 10 best online libraries

1 Internet Archive: the largest digital library
to download free ebooks.

2. Project Gutenberg: offers over 33,000 free ebooks.

3. Google Books: preview books then google will give
you a link to download the ebook if it's not
copyrighted.

4. University of Pennsylvania Books Page: lists over 1
million free books to read and download.

5. Open Library: over 1 million classic literature
free ebooks to download.

6. eBooks at Adelaide: , free classic literature,
philosophy, science and medicine ebooks.

7. Bartleby: provides the encyclopedia of world.

8. Bibliomania: offers over 2000
free electronic documents, as well as research results.

9. The New York Public Library: offers thousands of
free ebooks in various formats.

10. ManyBooks: ads free library to download over
29,000 free ebooks.

PENNY SMART

ORDER FORM

TO ORDER ADDITIONAL COPIES OF THIS BOOK

COST: $21.95 PLUS 13% HST (CANADA ONLY) & SHIPPING COST.

EMAIL: COOLRVING@GMAIL.COM

Subject Header: RV Living is Cool Book

Visit site: http://coolrving.com/ to place an order.

5 BOOKS & MORE 10% DISCOUNT
10 BOOKS & MORE 15% DISCOUNT

FOR LARGER VOLUMES, CUSTOMISED ORDERS EMAIL

PENNY SMART COOLRVING@GMAIL.COM

About the Author

Penny Smart is a fun internet geek, who loves being a Full-timer and a world traveller taking her virtual consulting practice everywhere using the internet since the mid 90's when she attended the world's first virtual trade mission in Malaysia hosted by IBM and the historical Women's International Trade Mission held in Washington DC. She loves the many RV adventures while travelling with her husband and their two pet Chihuahuas in their home on wheels.

Penny enjoys teaching adults how to use smartphones and iPads as an adjunct professor at a Canadian College and can be reached coolrving@gmail.com.

PENNY SMART

VALUABLE RESOURCES

CROSS BORDER INFORMATION

[i] CDN Nexus http://www.cbsa-asfc.gc.ca/cpr-crp-eng.html

[ii] US Nexus
http://usa.immigrationvisaforms.com/travel/nexus-pass

MOBILE OFFICE

[iii] GO TO MY PC http://www.gotomypc.com

[iv] WEB CONFERENCE http://www.webex.com/

[v] E VOICE http://www.evoice.com/

[vi] MY FAX http://www.myfax.com

[vii] http://beta.skype.com/en/

FREE CREDIT REPORT

[viii] EQUFAX http://www.equifax.com/answers/request-free-credit-report/en_cp

---

REFERENCE SOURCES

[ix] SMITHSONIAN http://www.smithsonianmag.com/history-archaeology/Commemorating-100-Years-of-the-RV.html

[x] WIKIPEDIA http://en.wikipedia.org/wiki/List_of_recreational_vehicles

MEMBERSHIPS

[xi] CAA http://www.caasco.com

[xii] AAA http://autoclubsouth.aaa.com

[xiii] GOOD SAM CLUB http://www.goodsamclub.com

[xiv] WOODALLS http://www.woodalls.com/

[xv] PASSPORT AMERICA http://www.passportamerica.com

ICLOUD DRIVES

[xvi] MSN SKYDRIVE www.**skydrive.com**

[xvii] GOOGLE DRIVE www.**googlegdrive**.com

[xviii] DROP BOX https://www.dropbox.com/

Penny Smart

PREPAID CELLULAR PLANS

[xix]CONSUMERCELLULARhttp://www.consumercellular.com/

[xx] MY SIMPLE MOBILE http://www.mysimplemobile.com/

[xxi] H2WIRELESS https://www.h2owirelessnow.com/

[xxii] KOODO http://koodomobile.com/en/on/index.shtml

[xxiii]VIRGIN http://www.virginmobile.ca/en/plans/prepaid-talktext-plans.html

FREE INTERNET PHONE

[xxiv] SKYPE http://www.skype.com

[xxv] PING http://www.pinger.com/content/home.html

INTERNET TV

[xxvi] NETFLIX https://signup.netflix.com/

[xxvii] HULU http://www.hulu.com/plus/content

RVing the Cool Lifestyle Way

RVER APPS

xxviii CAMP & RV APP http://www.allstays.com/

xxix CHEAP GAS https://itunes.apple.com/us/app/cheap-gas/id290765007?mt=8

xxx FLIPBOARD http://flipboard.com/

xxxi TUNEIN RADIO http://tunein.com/

xxxii TV TOWERhttp://appshopper.com/travel/tv-towers-usa

xxxiii WEATHERBUG http://weather.weatherbug.com/

xxxiv WALMART http://www.walmart.com/cp/Walmart-Mobile-App/1087865

xxxv JWIRE http://www.jiwire.com/iphone

xxxvi VALENTINE https://itunes.apple.com/us/app/valentine-radio/id302007784?mt=8

xxxvii KAMSUTRA http://kama-sutra-app.com/

xxxviii 50 SHADES OF GREY https://itunes.apple.com/us/app/trivia-for-fifty-shades-grey/id551903595?mt=8

PENNY SMART

MONEY SAVING APPS

[xxxix] AMAZON PRICE CHECK
http://www.amazon.com/gp/feature.html?ie=UTF8&docId=aw_ppricecheck_iphone_mobile

[xl] RED LASER http://mobile.ebay.com/iphone/redlaser

[xli] GROCERY LIST http://www.groceryiq.com/

[xlii] GROUPON http://www.groupon.com/mobile

[xliii] MINT https://www.mint.com/how-it-works/anywhere/iphone/

LOOKING FOR WORK

[xliv] CRAIGS LIST http://mobile.craigslist.org/

[xlv] JOB AWARE https://itunes.apple.com/us/app/jobaware-job-search-just-got/id453682011?mt=8

[xlvi] JOB SEARCH https://itunes.apple.com/us/app/job-search/id309735670?mt=8

[xlvii] INDEED http://www.indeed.com/mobile

[xlviii] WORKAMPER http://www.workamper.com/

[xlix] GURU http://www.guru.com/

---

[i] ELANCE https://www.elance.com

BEING SMARTER/EDUCATION

[li] COURSERA https://www.coursera.org/

[lii] EDX https://www.edx.org/

[liii] OPEN CULTURE FREE COURSES
http://www.openculture.com/freeonlinecourses

[liv]TED http://www.ted.com/

---

www.ingramcontent.com/pod-product-compliance
Lightning Source LLC
Chambersburg PA
CBHW021824170526
45157CB00007B/2683